Acclaim for *Chinese Blackbird*

"Who am I? Where do I fit in? From where will I draw my strength? By turns lyrical and fierce, the poems in *Chinese Blackbird* ask some of the essential questions of identity. Sherry Lee writes soulfully of the joy and pain of an examined life."

—Alison McGhee, Associate Professor,
Metropolitan State University
Author of novels, poetry and picture books for all ages

"Sherry's *Chinese Blackbird* is a double phoenix triumph. It's a triumph over the stories we hide about ourselves or the stories we're told we have to hide."

—Marlina Gonzalez, Programs Manager,
Intermedia Arts

"Sherry Quan Lee's books, *Chinese Blackbird* and *How to Write a Suicide Note* are evidence that writing helps to acknowledge and work through issues that affect women of color, especially biracial women. They are handbooks for writers who want guidance in the craft of writing; but, mostly they are books of hope."

—Lori Young-Williams, student
in Quan Lee's workshop, *Stories that Save Lives*

"Sherry Lee is a bold writer. Her work shines on the page. The way she tells her truths, her sharp eye for cultural details, for where passion and longing reside, her wit--all are in evidence on every page of *Chinese Blackbird*. I love the way her mind works, and her willingness to travel off expected paths in order to find the forms and the images she must have to make her art."

Deborah Keenan, poet, Professor,
Hamline University MFA program

"In *Chinese Blackbird*, Sherry Quan Lee renders stories of her complex cultural heritage with the lyrical touch of a poet coming into self-possession. In revealing herself in her poetry, Lee exhibits in no uncertain terms the following motto: "I write myself, therefore I am." As, Dr. Henry Louis Gates asserts in *Bearing Witness: Selections from African-American Autobiography in the Twentieth Century*, such a saying, "...could be taken as the motto of [African-African people] in this country." Lee, both African-American and Chinese, creates a work representing the U.S. Black literary tradition replete with autobiographies of Black writers, who birth, name and claim the self that has often been denied, stemming from the antebellum period of slavery to the postmodern era of the new millennium. Through the generative power of language, Lee creates an inspirational and a multifarious self. This self blows breath unto the page and into the reader, who may have felt quiescent or invisible, often feeling forced to choose among various enriching worlds, until she experiences the truth that only good literature can unveil about the joys and struggles of defining oneself on one's terms."

—Pamela R. Fletcher
Co-Director of Critical Studies in Race and Ethnicity
College of St. Catherine

Fletcher assigns Chinese Blackbird *every year in the literature courses she teaches in St. Paul, Minnesota. In these courses, intrigued students have considered "Dear M.F.A. Faculty" as one of the most notable poems in the collection. Word to the wise: M.F.A. students of color: consider it a cautionary tale.*

Sherry Quan Lee

Book #3 in the Reflections of America Series

Chinese Blackbird
Copyright © 2002, 2008 Sherry Quan Lee. All rights reserved

Editor
  Sun Yung Shin
Interior Design
  Liz Tufte, Folio Bookworks

Cover Design
  Holly Heewon Lee
Cover Photography
  Charissa Uemura

First Printing: March 2002 by Asian American Renaissance.
Second Printing: July 2008 by Modern History Press

Library of Congress Cataloging-in-Publication Data

Lee, Sherry, 1948-
  Chinese blackbird / Sherry Quan Lee.
     p. cm. -- (Reflections of America series ; bk. #3)
  ISBN-13: 978-1-932690-68-2 (trade paper : alk. paper)
  ISBN-10: 1-932690-68-9 (trade paper : alk. paper)
  1. Racially mixed children--Poetry. 2. Racially mixed women--Poetry. I. Title. II. Series.

PS3562.E3644C47 2008
811'.54--dc22

                                        2008022999

Published by: Modern History Press, an imprint of

Loving Healing Press
5145 Pontiac Trail
Ann Arbor, MI 48105
USA
http://www.LovingHealing.com or
info@LovingHealing.com
Fax +1 734 663 6861

Modern History Press

Reflections of America Series

The Stories of Devil-Girl by Anya Achtenberg

How to Write a Suicide Note: serial essays that saved a woman's life by Sherry Quan Lee

Chinese BlackBird by Sherry Quan Lee

"The *Reflections of America* Series highlights autobiography, fiction, and poetry which express the quest to discover one's context within modern society."

From Modern History Press

Preface

Taken as a whole, the poems in this book tell a story: A girl is born of a Chinese immigrant father and a black mother with a "passing jones." The father leaves and the mother encourages her children not to identify themselves as black. The girl grows up and encounters abuse and neglect, she battles with ignorance and racism, depression and suicidal urges. She goes through several marriages. She starts to write. She starts to ask questions about who she is, who her father was, who her mother was, about the heritages that have formed her. She raises her children and manages to help them to grow up with a buoyancy that she finds striking, given their heritages. She moves through the death of her parents, the death of a last marriage. She discovers her love of women; she falls in love with a woman. She survives and flounders and flourishes. She continues to ask questions about who she is, about the bewildering cruelties and beauty of the world around her. She continues to write, past doubt, past uncertainties, past rejection, past the official guardians of literature. She persists on her journey. She will not be silenced.

And after you finish this book you will say to yourself, if you have any sense at all, this woman is a hero. This book is a gift. This book is a small and powerful miracle. If you read it with an open mind and heart, it will tell you much about America; it will tell you truths that are not there in our culture of mass media or in our canonized literature. It will tell you how complicated a thing it is to grow up in this country as a person of color with a mixed racial and cultural heritage. It will tell how much silence there is around the desires of someone who loves those of the same sex. It will tell you how, for certain people, so very few tools are given to speak about their identity, to find out who they are. It will tell you how those tools can be constructed, poem by poem, line by line—only with honesty and courage, only with tenacity, only with a fierceness that will not give up. Poetry was not given to Sherry Quan Lee; she had to go out and find it. She had to fight for it.

The poems in this book run a wide gamut of tones—sometimes lyrical, sometimes wry and biting and caustic, sometimes passionate, sometimes grieving, sometimes angry. They often move quickly and contain surprising juxtapositions of imagery and tone. They are alive and highly cognizant of the ironies of the poet's experiences and her position in the world; they explore the misperceptions and censoring and condescensions and critiques and insults she has battled. At times there's a surprising ability to find humor in the midst of difficult and painful situations, and this comes in part because the poet does not take herself too seriously. At the same time, this is not a wit that comes from distance or safety; it's a wit created out of and within adversity. At certain points, there's an aphoristic quality to the lines, a bit of wisdom or truth distilled and wrestled from experience.

> *Sometimes I feel like a boxer punching myself.*
> *I reverberate.*
> *The good thing is, some things shake loose.*

Overall there's an emotional honesty in these poems that I trust. I'm struck by how vulnerable this poet is, how willing she is to look at the pain inside her and around her with open eyes, unflinching. She knows that words cannot erase wounds but they do allow them to heal: "I turn my bruises into stories/ and watch them disappear."

Like any reader, I have my own particular favorite individual poems in this book; they include *Dear M.F.A. Faculty, Parthenogenesis, Chokecherry, Theun Wing, Vampire, Naming*. But the individual poems also gather themselves up into something larger; they gain power from the vision and voice that they come together to form. Unlike so many volumes of poetry, at the end of this book you will leave with a strong sense of who this poet, who this woman, is. You will feel as if you have encountered a very real and complicated individual, a person who has made her descent into the underworld, as good writers must, and come back with her own particular vision, one balancing darkness with the light of articulation and the passion for clarity. You will feel a certain wonder and awe that one person has gone through so much and not only come through it, but has come forward to tell her tale.

—David Mura

IN MEMORY of MY MOTHER
Mom, I Miss You

Sarah Ella Franklin Quan
1913-1999

Acknowledgements

I have been *writing for my life* since I left my mother's house when I was eighteen. It was a house with a white picket fence that protected me from who I was: Chinese, Black, and Female. But there are no boundaries to hold the emotional traumas of *longing, shame, and terror* that Toi Derricotte so courageously speaks about in *the black notebooks*. But, writing and revealing are, for me, acts of freedom, forgiveness, and love that also have no boundaries. Ironically, I have also been *running for my life* . . . away from me instead of toward me. Somewhere between the birth of my children and menopause (the pause of men, according to my friend Kris) I have run into myself. We're still getting acquainted, but we're not afraid.

Chinese Blackbird could not have happened without the support of the Asian American Renaissance. Elsa J. Batica, Executive Director of AAR, has encouraged me from her first day on the job—*just find a way to do it, and we'll do it*! David Mura, former Artistic Director of AAR, has been my mentor as facilitator of the Writer's Block Program for Asian American youth, as mentor for the Loft Literary Center's Asian Pacific Inroads Program, and as personal mentor he helped me discover the narrative that flows through my poems which became the backbone of *Chinese Blackbird*.

Chinese Blackbird could not have happened without my teachers who understood the subtleties and complexities of my writing and my life. Special thanks to Nikki Giovanni, Linda Hogan, Nelly Wong, Deborah Keenan, Toi Derricotte, Alexs Pate, and David Mura.

Chinese Blackbird could not have happened without the Asian American Renaissance; SASE: The Write Place; Unbound: Asian Women Write! and Cave Canem, a writing retreat for Black poets founded by Toi Derricotte and Cornelius Eady.

Chinese Blackbird could not have happened without Dr. Nancy "Rusty" Barceló—and her insistence that it should happen. I thank you *Rusty* for all of your *nos and all of your yeses.*

Chinese Blackbird could not have happened without my family who understood the fear, the anger, and the heartache. They encouraged me to share our stories—Aunt Grace, Aunt Marion, Cousin Terri, Niece Stacy Lee Quan, and Sons Michael and David. Thank you.

Chinese Blackbird could not have happened without my siblings. Whether we sidestep, hover over, or embrace each other, we know forgiveness and we know love.

Chinese Blackbird could not have happened without my friends and mentors—Eden Torres, Carolyn Holbrook, Beth Kyong Lo, Sun Yung Shin, Barb Bergeron, Corrine Young, Jane Swatosh, Holly Hee Won Coughlin, Lupé Castillo, Kathy Regalado, Lynn Fisher, Kris Frykman, Lee Orcutt, Vidhya Shanker, Annie Hoffman, Denice Leverett, Mary Jane Madden, Bonnie Brazzale, Rosina Merchant Lane, Renee Moore, Valerie Jean, and Charissa Uemura.

Chinese Blackbird could not have happened without Sun Yung Shin's keen editing, her sense of how changing one word or a line break can make surprising changes in tone, rhythm, and meaning. And special thanks to Holly Hee Won Coughlin for a cover design that is meaningful and inviting.

Chinese Blackbird could not have happened without everyone that has ever touched my life. I often quote from Nikki Giovanni's poem, *When I Die: —and if ever I touched a life I hope that life knows / that I know that touching was and still is and will always / be the true / revolution.*

CONTENTS

NOT HIDING NOT WHITE
Chinese/Black/Woman   3
Wintergreen   4
Hocus-Pocus   6
Black Beauty Blues   7
Magnolia Café   8
Dear M.F.A. Faculty   9
Job Interview Number One After Earning An M.F.A.   12
Theory   13
Incarnation   15

CHINESE BLACKBIRD
Parthenogenesis   18
Chokecherry   20
Needles and Pins   22
Theun Wing   24
Glossolalia   25
Winter Solstice   26
Chinese Blackbird   28
Since I Was Born   29

ANXIETY WHERE ARE YOU? OH WELL, GOODBYE
Mother's and Mine   34
Reunion   39
Sixteen-Year-Old Vampire   44
Mazatlan, Spring Break   46
A Love Poem   47
Early Retirement   49
Wishing Well   51
This Breast Belongs to Me   53
Death, Divorce, Resurrection   54

DIVA BREAKIN' THE BLUES

China Doll   58
I Will Divorce You   59
Diva Breakin' the Blues   60
Women Who Run   61
It Is Not Good   63
Naming   64
Insomnia   66
What Song is She Singing?   68
I Asked My Husband If He Thought I Was A Lesbian
And He Said, Yes   70
Marathon   75
I Am the Snake I Feared   77

Not Hiding
Not White

Chinese/Black/Woman

I am pregnant with myself
gestation: fifty years.
I will come out standing on my head
knowing truth is upside down.
No one will slap this Chinese /
Black / Woman or proclaim
her identity. I will pass out (pink,
blue) cigars. Celebrate.
Perfection.

Wintergreen

Minnesota is not compatible
to my growth, it is too cold.

The Ice Age made it clear
*Magnolias, you can live
here in SE China, here in Georgia.*

My ancestors oppose the heat.

Civil wars and death—or just a robin
traveling against the season—
tossed Black / tossed Chinese:

Here I am, a Minnesota mutant.
Snowflake.

Like a magnolia, I am
not white.   It is only light
passing through.   Mama
cooked tuna noodle casserole
and Daddy ate it.

Like a magnolia
—whose sepals never fuse—
my life is disparate
               here a Black
               community,

        there an Asian
        community,
                       everywhere, white.

He who chops down Magnolia trees is
not a horticulturist
historian or
healer.

I am almost ripe.
Taste wintergreen.
Soon, I will *unzip* myself
shed pollen,

Flower

Hocus-Pocus

Mother cooked a white rabbit
in a black pot

abracadabra

mixed it with white rice
ate it with chopsticks

abracadabra

I put it in the garbage disposal
waved my hand

abracadabra

now you see me, now you

don't, in the nursing home
I feed mother black-eyed peas

she still can't swallow, even
with a stainless steel fork

I couldn't eat
white

Black Beauty Blues

Who knew

Mother

curled thick hair thin.

Singed the lie.

Red hot metal over gas flames.

Petroleum jelly a kitchen aid.

The kitchen always sterile

always white.

Magnolia Café

We ate red beans and rice, blackened catfish with hot pepper sauce, and drank lemon water. The conversation flip-flopped—graduate school, marijuana, poetry. She said Vanessa Williams didn't become Black until she lost the Miss America title and she is still only Black when she needs to be; and, of course, O.J. has never been Black. I had been questioning my own Blackness all weekend at the Celebration of Black Writing Conference—what is Black? Skin? Attitude? Language? Hair? The Black manager at our local *specializes in ethnic hair* salon said I don't have Black hair, who told me that I did? *Mama*, I tried to say, but before I could my Black friend, her hair in dreadlocks, screamed, *who are you to say my friend isn't Black? She has hair just like my mom's. Are you saying my mom isn't Black?* All those Minnesota ladies in-and-out of the tanning booth gettin' in earful. *Her hair might be Mixed, but it certainly isn't Black*—were they talking about hair or the color of my skin? What is Black? Are there membership dues and don'ts? My culture is White—Mama had a passin' jones. My ethnicity is multi-complex. People assume I am Italian, Puerto Rican, Mexican, Native American, etc. I speak the truth, Black, but I lack credibility. Perhaps I should only eat at Asian restaurants, or better yet, Ole and Lena's Pancake House.

Yesterday I braided my mama's hair. Lenore, who works at Mama's nursing home, asked Mama, *you look Indian, what are you?* I knew Mama wasn't going to respond, so after a long pause I said, *she's Black*.

I had to undo the braid before Mama would go down to the cafeteria for watermelon. What is Black? One drop or a gallon? A popularity contest? A poor me contest? Can you have money and still be Black? Be educated and still be Black? Have a Chinese father and still be Black? Have an Irish great-grandfather son of a plantation owner and still be Black? Black or not, can I still eat red beans and rice?

Dear M.F.A. Faculty

Thank you for correcting typos
on my M.F.A. final project
and my twenty-book essay
examination. By the way,
Amiri Baraka and Amina Baraka
were not misspelled, she and he
do not have the same first name.
But, thank you for being *concerned*
about my *carelessness*.

You are correct, however, I
had *no apparent sense* that I
landed my essay with a cliche.
Metaphorically speaking, I
was flying in the dark.

I'm glad you like my phrase: *well,
how many colorful women are white-
washed in South Scandinavian
Minneapolis*—however, you did misquote
me. I did not spell colorful COLOURFUL.

(Incidentally, the comma goes inside
the quotation mark, and quotation
marks look like this: "   .")

Thank you for *judging*
the use of my quotes
    on the whole
as accurate. Thank you
for stating that my phrases
make [you] like [me].

Should I have known
this was a popularity contest?
I'm sorry I didn't include
a centerfold. But a photo
wouldn't have revealed my
racial identity.

Thank you for respecting
my *unsuccessful attempt*
at the non-linear.
Although you insist
it takes *more skill* to achieve the non-
linear, I believe it takes more
living.

Actually, I didn't know
I was writing a non-linear essay—
I merely, apparently, wrote a bad five paragraph essay
in which case your contempt
could be justified.

I'm sorry my conscious
attempt
to use academic vernacular
did not terminate the *incredulous* mistake
which caused you to *lose
patience*.

Of the three *anonymous* critiques
two were condenscending
and the other so patronizing
I framed it.

Don't you think it's amazing
that you passed me
on the M.F.A. Essay Exam and
accepted my final M.F.A. Project
as proof of earning
a graduate degree?

Did you know my final g.p.a.
is 4.0?

And do you know
I am Black/Chinese?

Job Interview Number One After Earning an M.F.A. Degree in English/Creative Writing

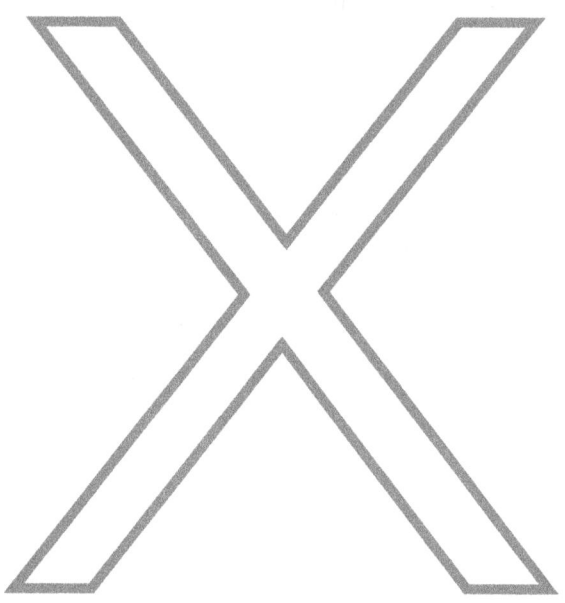

Theory

1.
At universities scientists and artists argue—fiction or non-fiction? Historians lie. Truth is only one professor's assumption based on another professor's assumption, based on a dead professor's assumption.

Not too much is new.

But for every colorful woman, there is a first time. First kiss, first rape, first home, first homelessness, (first husband), (first son), (first woman), first love, first death—Mother's death.

Each woman's story wrapped in someone else's words, typed according to MLA or APA guidelines, and hung from holiday trees, symmetrically balanced, pretty decorations. Shiny, reflective, glorious.

Safe.

2.
I took the silver ornaments off my tree before my fiftieth birthday. Holidays tarnish like mirrors.

I avoid mirrors. Stay away from bathrooms, dressing rooms, cosmetic counters.

3.
Death. Finally, Mom no longer has to look in mirrors. Begotten of children begotten of children begotten of plantation lust and demand. Sometimes it's about rape. Sometimes it's about rape.

When will our resurrection come?

4.
I have always been blessed with chancre sores. My mouth repels
my voice.

My mouth says stop.

I hold in too much history. My lungs are coated. My stomach fat.

The sores disappear after breathing in, breathing out. After
a couple of good weeks of untying lies, my body and soul are clean
for the length of a woman's cycle.

I will not rust.

5.
I have tried to write my experience based on someone else's theory.
It keeps coming out poetry.

6.
I saw my mother grow large. Larger than her fetal position.
Larger than her broken bones. Larger than her black and blue
bruises.

Covered with white hospital sheets, not hiding, not white.

Incarnation

Father escaped mother with his chow mein
and the flaming red-haired woman who

served it to him. Mother remained starched
white rice steaming in a black

kettle. Jesus was at the Lutheran church
across the street—I had access

to him *this white light of mine; I'm gonna let it shine
let it shine 'til Jesus comes; this white light*

of mine No one knew, Jesus and I weren't white
each of us conceived—immaculately.

Hungry for sweet potato pie and string bean chop suey,
I jumped the fence the neighborhood, the city.

At a monastery in New York I confess to a priest,
and twenty-seven poets that I am Black

and they, the Cave Canem poets, respond, *Amen.*
Sticky Rice, publishes my poem, "White Dragon"

no one says: *you're not Asian.*
I shave my head. Thank you Nikki Giovanni,

Sapphire, Ndegeocello. I am a Buddhist
nun, burn the chapters of my memoir
                                        one by one.

Chinese Blackbird

Parthenogenesis

1.
Mama swears
she didn't have sex
with her husband
after my sister Sheila was born—
abracadabra Dad disappeared
      but, I arrived ten months later

2.
the whip-tailed lizard
and the dandelion
also, are sperm free,
the water flea says yes when it needs to
and mollies just need stimulation

3.
Scientists claim sex is a mystery.
I like a good mystery—

a friend asked, *If your dad isn't
your father, how can you be Chinese?*

I replied, *If my great-grandfather is white,
how can I be Black?*

4.
My mother is Sara Kali.

5.
Am I a woman or
a man? What gender is
Jesus?

In spite of mythology, Virgin
births will always be

daughters, but couldn't I be the son
Father almost waited for

if only he had used his imagination
instead of his magic

Abracadabra

Chokecherry

I am a yellow-bellied
blackbird
churning chokecherries.

Shit white. Spring ripe.
Christ resurrected.
The cross, red.

Mama who is Black
danced
an Irish jig.

The plantation owner's son
courted
great-grandma with a pig.

I remember singing

> *Bye-bye black bird*

Mama's siblings dodged
Mama's neighbors
Mama's fears;

invited us to their homes
with blinds open.

The Mississippi river flows
South.
> *Black bird, black bird*
fly away home?

Grandma wouldn't eat ham. Mama won't
eat chitlins.

Yellow-bellied blackbird
chokes.

Needles and Pins

Mom has not slimmed down
she carries the weight of five white children

at seventy her skin hangs loose
unattached to any black heritage

Father left after 18 years of marriage
gambled on the white, red-haired woman

he met at work, abandoned all things Chinese
the plastic-tiled mah jong set,

the newly conceived son

Mom taught four girls to build
walls, bet on white dragons,

her ivory wall trespassed only at night
black relatives out of sight

of Scandinavian neighbors,
children asleep, unable to ask

questions / we never questioned white
dolls in pink dresses

our dresses red taffeta with white lace collars
mother bound four girls with silk thread

how could she make us exotic, desired?
our brother was on his own, identity

not held taut with patterns and pins

he owned thirteen cars the year he turned sixteen
sped down dirt roads, transgressed white

picket fences. Girls: we could not
stray, locked

in a house on a hill
we were fed ginseng—ripened for the right man

Mother had faith *with God all things are*
possible and the planchette moved across our Ouija board

in agreement. She watched
as we danced on the living room carpet

muttered holy petitions, but there were no future
husbands in our neighborhood. She doesn't believe

that Elvis is dead, or that some of the men we married
spit nails at us.

she taught us to wear pale pink
make-up—hide puncture wounds, camouflage
pain, and keep
                strutting

Mother is immune—virgin, goddess. In her one room
high-rise she reads Harlequin romance novels.

My sisters and I rip out the tight stitches, laugh
about the alcohol, the men. Our brother experiments
with needles

Theun Wing

Father was a model minority
>   *Jesus Loves the Little Children*
assimilation fit
>   *red and yellow black and white*
like a baseball glove

he earned straight As. Stopped speaking
>   *Jesus Loves the Little Children*
Chinese. Fought the Japanese
in WW II. He said *no*

to a Chinese Bride
married my mother
>   *red and yellow black and white*
a Negro. I carry his life
between lies.

I saw him five times
>   *Jesus Loves the Little Children*
in forty-five years, never knew
if I missed him. When he died

I sent flowers. Sympathy
>   to the Polish wife,
>>   the children I never
red and yellow black and white
>>>   met. Mourned him in Chinatown, San Francisco
with other dead Chinese
>   men I didn't know

Glossolalia

She discarded Martin Luther,
never was attached to any pope,
the Episcopal priest
was a one-night affair. Born
again, she trashed idle
objects: men—
  and the brass Buddha.

Her nightmares stopped,
but she still couldn't speak
in tongues. Like Emily
she stopped going to church,
spent Sundays at home.

Father's obituary read, *survived
by wife and children.* The wife
wasn't her mother. The children
weren't her siblings.

The brass Buddha can't
be resurrected.

There are no prophets, just
plump men and dead fathers
with tarnished bellies.

Winter Solstice

December there was no snow
to blanket us in whiteness, no cold
to freeze the truth.
Apparitions of past holidays sauntered
nostalgically, siblings wandered
bumping into each other.
Our customary dark countenance
recanted.

Death of our father was more relief
than sorrow, he had been dead
since the divorce.
He never made the trip home
to see his mother in China. News
of his death
sent our Mother to the hospital
     oxygen in portable tanks
     assisted
until she could breathe
independently, at last, after 42 years—

she was free

we were surprised at how much she wanted
to live. For the first time, she told us
we were beautiful.

We let go of our secrets, pausing
from the chaos of colored lines,
hiding alcohol, needles, and pills,
past lovers, and husbands;
we all had some kind of an addiction,
none of us had self-esteem.

Memories escaped from the house
we lived in as naive children
(we thought we were Scandinavian).

It wasn't the yin and the yang of balance
that I felt, but better,
the smashing together and destruction
of incongruities.

Chinese Blackbird

This woman has wings.
Tear shaped.
                Slivers of silver,
                slick strands of DNA—
                              feathers ruffled.

The wings of this woman.
Tear shaped.
                Amnesia temporary.

                        You are not white. White
                        is a parody, passing.

Winged. This woman.
Tear shaped.
                Flight canceled.

Father is dead. Mother
senile.

        This woman's wings.
        Tear shaped.
                          Perched on a limb
                          she sings, on a limb
                          she sings.

Woman! Wings! Chinese /
Black
       bird. Black/

bird. Chinese.

        Her parents'
        desire.

Since I Was Born

Doesn't everyone have some place to go
and a reason for going there?

Where are you now, Mother?

Are we at our house
in South Scandinavian
Minneapolis?

Are we sitting on red vinyl chairs
at a gray Formica table?

Have you dunked your Zwieback toast
in your cup of Hills Brothers Coffee?

Has my gingersnap crumbled in my milk?

Or are we older? You with yet another State Fair yardstick
in your hand?

Me crying. You swatting.
Me screaming.

It wasn't a game, mother.
I really didn't know why
I was crying—
              (I didn't know you
and I
        are female and Black).

Or are we younger? Years one through four, lost
like my Chinese father to memory?

Is it too late to break, silence?

My own fingers have never felt
the woman I am. Have never sensed
anything but hard rejection.

Have never made me smile.

I am dark vanilla.
How have I hurt myself?
    . . .

You said I couldn't join the Navy.
Were you afraid
of women wanting me?
Or were you afraid

I might want a woman?

Am I the woman I'm in love with?

    . . .

We are not a mistake.

I cradle her songs in the palm
of my fears, and

discover my prayers.

    . . .

I tried suicide three times.
So long ago.

It was my time to die.

My brother punctured a vein
with an amphetamine pistol

I stuck a hard pencil and a soft
penis in my mouth

my crosses, white men
and marriage.

. . .

I say I am bleeding.
Tighten the tourniquet.

A few lost limbs can't hurt
arms and legs belong

to ancestors I don't know—
Black women and Chinese men.

. . .

What change of life is this?
What makes me refuse

to apologize? Why can't
I lie flat, starched—

that paper doll I let everyone
dress?

Amputation is painful, still
sometimes necessary

healing, howling.

I don't want to die.

. . .

I am my mother's daughter
my father's son.

I'm not giving in
to some other woman's trauma—

and that scares me

Anxiety Where Are You? Oh Well, Goodbye

Mother's and Mine

1.
Mother lived to be eighty-six years old. I'll be damned if every lifetime bruise didn't show itself on her predeath body. They were big bruises. And grew larger as I watched her die. I didn't bother to count them. I've been counting them every day since I was born. They were black and they were blue.

2.
I no longer look for the answers. Asking the questions is enough.

3.
After death do bruises disappear? The doctor said Mom had a leukemia blast. This after he and we all agreed leukemia wasn't what was killing her. Wasn't what would kill her. Black was the color Mother crushed. Or did it crush her? Mother, white is not a color. Your sisters dealt with Black in other ways-marrying it, cursing it, celebrating it. Purple is the woman I have become.

4.
Where is it I want to go? Mother went to a one-room high rise. Went to her room and locked the door. Sometimes I knocked. Once in awhile she answered. Responding most favorably to chocolate kisses, romance novels, and lottery tickets.

5.
Bruises are painful, colorful reminders that one has been hit. Or has walked into foreign objects. I run away again and again. Open the first door I see and slam into dysfunction. Mother, is it you I keep running into?

6.
Mother, what is it I haven't yet recognized? What gifts did you try to give me? If, from wherever you are now, you could make my bruises go away, would you?

7.
Mother wanted me married. She wanted the white lieutenant to sing his way out of South Pacific and marry all three of her Chinese daughters. Did she know I might prefer Liat? Why, Mother, did you want for your daughters that which you refused for yourself? What was it about my father that disappointed you? Bloody Mary chewed betel nuts. Where was her husband?

8.
My friend says she's a trauma drama queen. I said, "you're not." I thought, "Is that what I am—a trauma drama queen?" Sounds flamboyant. Sounds self-serving. Sounds tiring. How many times have I run away?

9.
Happiness is an emotion. A damn good one. I've decided to be happy.

10.
How can I explain this happiness, this wealth of bruises? My hands hurt. My legs are stiff. I have a headache.

11.
And still, another bruise won't let me sleep. I can't see it. I can't name it. Did I forget to say, "I'm sorry"? If I didn't say, "I'm sorry," is it too late? *Mom, I miss you.*

12.
I was afraid the things you told me when I was a child were true. The bag of bones in the basement and the butter man. The shoemaker. The high school boy. But, why were you afraid of the women? Your sisters, the neighbor ladies, and your daughters?

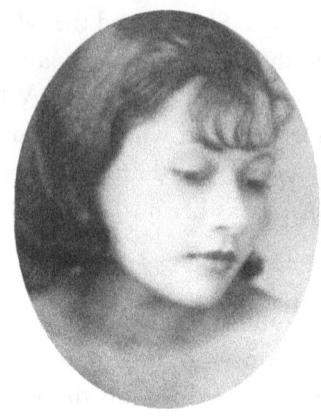

13.
Sometimes I feel like a boxer punching myself. I reverberate. The good thing is, some things shake loose. *Mom, I'm sorry I ran away.*

14.
Maybe I should go to the basement and throw away more of who I am not.

15.
A big bruise is centered in my belly. The world is heavy. Like stale gum chewed and forgotten. A wad in the mouth in the morning. I am fifty-two years old and breathing heavy. Is there anything wrong with desire? When I lie down in bed, I drool. A slobbering idiot I've become. Sometimes, I just wake up sad.

16.
I know when the bruise is dormant. It watches. It listens. I know. But I forget.

17.
I always loved my mother.

18.
Perhaps I am happy because death is just a sunrise or two away and it must be beautiful. Or perhaps I am happy because I am not dead. Anxiety, where are you? Oh well, goodbye.

19.
When I stopped wanting what I couldn't have, I bruised less often. When I stopped beating myself up because ugly and stupid were words I made up, my vocabulary grew and I bruised less often. When I stopped lashing out, I bruised less often. When I stopped acquiescing, I bruised less often. When I stopped all the lies, I bruised less often. When I realized how much I loved women, men were suddenly human and I bruised less often.

20.
I pay attention to my bruises, turn them into stories and watch them disappear.

21.
A bruise is temporary. The dent in the car. The pinch in the butt. The sixteen-year-old son. The blank page. A bruise appears. Disappears. No stitches. No scars. No attachments.
No prolonged anger. No hate.

22.
There are flowers everywhere and birds. Bamboo plants and tiger lilies. A cardinal this morning. My garden is a small room. Bruises are beautiful. They are not harmful. They are not slit wrists, overdoses of drugs, a hung rope. I have given up poison. Cigarettes. Bologna. Self-doubt. Scotch. My prayers are no longer petitions, but praise. Tomorrow I might stumble.
The bruise will be beautiful. Love is so easy.

23.
Bruises are like lilacs. Beautiful in bloom, and seasonal.

24.
Mother hit me. I was prepubescent, a crying girl. The yardstick broke into splinters of heartache. Mother's and mine. It was all about love. Mother couldn't say she wanted it. She couldn't risk her daughter wanting it. She had many yardsticks. Is death opportunity or loss?

25.
Father wanted to be Western. Wanted America. Though his long trip on the U.S.S. China wasn't his choice, he made it his reality. Where is my father's boat now? I want to get on it. I want to return to a place neither of us knows. But, I won't leave in chaos. I won't leave crying or screaming. I won't leave questions unanswered. I won't leave not knowing where I'm going.

26.
The answer must be in the words of my dying mother: "Get out of my hospital room. I want to be alone."

27.
The answer must be in the words of my response: "I love you. I am not leaving. I know who I am."

28.
My bruises are the love I keep running away from.

Reunion

I love women, even though I've always married men. I love my sisters—all over fifty. Our lives started in the west, traveled south, and are now east—a half-circle headed north, curving like the soft skin embracing our bodies. Never a straight line. We meandered in and out of each other's lives, twisted in personal dramas we thought would never end.

Summer Solstice

My sister Sheila left Arizona on the evening of summer solstice. Thus began the joining of lost family, sisters once sliced into necessary pieces of a sour grapefruit, searching for the sugar that would sweeten our lives. At first, I didn't know what was happening. I anticipated summer alone—a season with no intruders. Meditating in a garden of sweet smelling lilacs. Reading. Writing. The audacity of my sister to fly like a crow to Minneapolis with no luggage but her pent-up anxieties!

Now, not only my sister, but her husband, too, lived in my basement. Their presence reminded me of the ghost that lived in our basement when we were children:

> *coming up one step bumpity-bump, coming up two steps bumpity-bump, coming up three steps bumpity bump, coming up four steps bumpity-bump. Now I'm in the kitchen, bumpity-bump. Now I'm in the living room, bumpity-bump. Now I'm in the bedroom, bumpity-bump. And, now I've got you!*

The Wedding

My niece, Little Sallie Jean Jelly Bean, marries in a Polish Catholic church in Northeast Minneapolis. Pierogies and fortune cookies. Polka and rock and roll. My sisters and I sit together and talk. For a change, this wedding isn't one of ours. This is definitely our year of coming full circle. Our year of attachment.

We are four little girls playing telephone. Messages whispered, words jumbled, sentences smashed. Our laughter connects us like paper dolls, the kind you make by folding paper and cutting toward the fold. When you open the paper there is a row of identical dolls holding hands. Four middle-aged women with short, gray hair.

Who we had been, women struggling toward maturity, was invisible. We were in the present. Only our catharsis marked us. Big Sallie hadn't brought her camera. A small sign, but a significant one as she let go of caretaking and control. The oldest of five siblings, Sallie had been the crutch my mother leaned on. When Dad left—the sixth grader we all leaned on. Today Sheila has the camera, and we all take turns taking pictures.

The photograph a guest takes of the four Quan girls is blurred. The camera isn't out of focus. Ironically, we posed ourselves off-balance. Unconsciously. Perhaps mocking our past lives. We are all smiling. We hold each other, our arms wrapped around one another's waists. One of us is wearing turquoise, one is wearing red, one chartreuse, and one purple.

We go to my house after the wedding. I put a turkey in the oven and rice in the rice cooker. Some things from the past are recycled. The joy of eating together, for example.

The Duncan Phyfe table in our childhood dining room had always been the center of Quan family rituals. That's where we shuffled Mah Jong tiles on hot summer afternoons. That's where Mom pinned and cut the identical clothes she sewed for four very different daughters. That's where we laid hands on the Ouija board, asking if the boys next door loved us or not. Most importantly, the Duncan Phyfe is where we ate our Sunday meals no later than noon. Roast beef or turkey or Swiss steak or pork chops, but always rice and gravy and Musselman's apple sauce. Until, of course, my older sisters started to invite boyfriends for Sunday dinner. Then we added mashed potatoes to our meal!

This Sunday afternoon I cook only rice. Kokuho Rose rice. Sticky rice. The rice that holds the Quan girls in sync.

My sisters arrive, this one or that one having stayed to dance one more dance, to listen to "Shout" or "Joy to the World." The game of telephone continues. We no longer whisper. We are loud and irreverent. We take off our tight shoes, and change into loose fitting t-shirts and shorts. We sprawl out on the love seats, the rocking chair, and the floor. My house is a mess—clothes and shoes everywhere—and discarded wedding programs. We are tired, content.

We don't dwell on the twists and the turns in our lives that sometimes separated us. Contortionists trying to escape home and fit into the world—Ohio, Colorado, California, Arizona, Illinois, Massachusetts, Washington. Some magic is only deception, the heart can be fooled. United states don't have crisis-free boundaries. Which one of us tried to commit suicide—three times? Who was addicted to amphetamines? One of us has scleroderma. Whose child is left physically challenged after a car accident. Which husband was a drunk, and abusive? Which husband refused to admit we are Black and invented Polynesian? Not all of our lovers left because we wanted them to. Who has had the same job for thirty-five years? Who has had thirty-five jobs?

We reminisce about the humor of our lives—sitcom tragedies. Four sisters—fourteen husbands! We laugh about getting drunk and falling off a barstool. Whose bartender boyfriend wouldn't give which one of us last call for alcohol? We laugh about how much they all loved us. Which boyfriend sat on the garage roof crying, upset that he had been dumped? We laugh about loving Theodorakis, Charlie Rich, Ted Neeley, Carl Anderson, and the Temptations. We consider having a party and inviting all the men we ever loved.

September 1997

As I sit in my sister Sheila's apartment, furnished with dishes and linens and beds from her sisters' basements and attics, along with garage-sale and thrift store treasures, I have almost forgotten the abrupt intrusion of her stomp into my life and interruption of my summer. She is the sister whose dark skin and straight hair were never a source of shame or to be questioned or compared, like my lighter skin and frizzy hair were for me. Yet, there was something that made her itch, that made her scratch. The scars on her arms and legs are just now beginning to heal. She never liked water, so when she was told to take her weekly bath, she ran the water, sat on the side of the tub, and dangled her toes. I wanted to take a bath every day, was ashamed that I couldn't. Who knows what the idiosyncrasies of our lives mean?

Sheila, my sister Susie, my sister Sallie, and I hold fifty-cent crystal wineglasses filled with May wine—the wine we drank in the seventies because it contained woodruff, supposedly a drug. We reminisce about my good-girl persona that kept me from doing acid or smoking marijuana. The persona that was simply a screen for my fear of being busted. My fear that someone would know I felt stupid, ugly, and unloved. A persona that couldn't hide my promiscuous search for the fairy-tale romance. We regale each other with stories that challenge our memories and our innocence. We admit that sex is as hallucinatory as LSD.

My sisters and I connect despite disparate experiences. Images of historic places and faces and fashions highlight a map. Each of us chooses our own color crayon to outline our separate journeys. It is clear where our lives intersect, meander, intersect again. We have created our own Monopoly game. Sometimes we land in jail together, sometimes we languish there alone. We pass "go" many times. Land on "free parking" less often, collect our fortunes and spend them.

It is late. We call it quits for the night. We smell like the potpourri of perennials in full bloom. We are seasoned, our roots deep. Weeds dead or dying. We go home, each to our own bed, or not.

As our hearts get old, we start to protect them—less fat, less cholesterol. And something delicious happens. Something to do with sensory perception. We pay attention. Qi-Gong is not just a word in an alternative journal.

Fifty as negative or old is a cultural, arbitrary phenomenon. I like being fifty. I know now, my over-fifty sisters and I could never escape each other; home is a single pushpin on a Minnesota map. We are a poem, a portrait. Miniature. There was never room for large gaps. We never traveled far. Minor detours were only minutes away from South Minneapolis.

Sixteen-Year-Old Vampire

-1-

He couldn't sleep. He needed
to eat. He sucked bloody images
on Nintendo
and bit into late night
MTV.

-2-

Daily I christened him
with a pitcher of cold water
and a glut of profanity
I tickled his feet and pulled
on his sheets, but
couldn't wake him.

-3-

Sometimes I imagined
he made it to school
on time, and stayed
awake during classes.

-4-

The psychologist and
the principal said,
"let go, it's his coffin."
I insisted he would graduate.

-5-

Perhaps I should have been
more reactionary. Baptized
him with holy water. Illuminated
his room with candles, or
made a bargain with the devil.

Instead, I wore a necklace of garlic,
and carried my rosary.

-6-

He never bit me in the neck
but often he howled,
fangs exposed.

He said *"get a life,
you're not Anne Rice."*

Mazatlan, Spring Break

Mother said, *no*,
you're not going to Mexico
end of conversation.

At the last minute,
father said, *why not?*—and paid
for his plane ticket.

Eighteen years old,
he slammed tequila shooters
all night,
vomited in the morning.

Too shy to love
the women he danced with
the Prince
wanting to be Charming
rescued an iguana—
bought it on the beach
for $10.00.

He didn't know
that borders restrict,
some lines can't be crossed,
iguanas can't leave Mexico.

He kissed his iguana goodbye

sometimes, fairy tales end abruptly

the iguana bit his salty lips.

Do lizards want to be loved?
or, does love cost more
than $10.00?

A Love Poem

This poem cost
$200.00, my husband
is not happy.

He is tiring, full
of a 22 oz. porterhouse.

Blues.

      Jazz.

            The wine is

French / I switch

to the house red
when the bottle is empty.

I want to stay, this is

my fifth poem \ scribbled
on paper napkins

(the wait person grabbed
the linen away from me).

I want to stay, it's
the first time I believe

I can write / but
my husband
has paid

　　　　　I love my husband.　But

　　　now it is time

　　　　　　　　to go.

　　　　　　　　　　　I am ready.

Early Retirement

I.

-a-

It wasn't breakfast in bed she smelled
only her desire for it. Nothing hot
under the sheets but her imagination;
she realized retirement is not always
voluntary, vacations are not always
satisfying. You can only buy
so many hand-painted Buddhas,
so many teapots.

-b-

What possessed him to caress
her breasts,   scrunch them
one at a time
through her oversized t-shirt,
she in the driver's seat,
hands on the wheel of their Winnebago
hoping to get home
before dark?

-c-

Their own bed wouldn't make
any difference, they bought
and washed fewer sheets. It wasn't
a temporary loss of memory, he
wouldn't be returning to work.
They were old, and, yes,
cynical, but they weren't
dead. They stopped at Super
America, bought maps of Seattle,
New Orleans, San Jose.

II.
       -a-
He pulls the fat straps
of her black knit tunic
off her shoulders
knowing she still goes braless
knowing her breasts are starting to sag
knowing the dress clings to her hips,
clings to her buttocks
in the heat and humidity
of this August afternoon.

           -b-
Perhaps the loose
leopard print slip
purchased at the Arizona flea market
is not seductive
still she dreams
of red roses
on the soft mattress—
of their Winnebago bed, instead

          -c-
"You're snoring," she says.

Wishing Well

I.

Intellectually,
I like warm
 breasts
better than a hard
 penis; yet,
during puberty
I had no intellect—
just innocent
 curiosity;
when I first came
to you
I was still naive.

If only I could flip-
flop a coin
and get an answer.

Last night,
on a Hollywood movie
a psychiatrist theorized
only women can achieve intimacy because men don't let go of life as a debate

and

enter it as a conversation.

II.

Sperm die quickly.
No wonder I never stay
fulfilled.

I must consummate

ecstasy alone.

Babies don't suck
 on daddy's penis;
a woman's breast
 provides nourishment.

I am what (you won't admit) you want

when I stop kow-towing to you
	with no interest
	or intimate paybacks.

This Breast Belongs to Me

*Received in the fresh state and labeled left breast
biopsy is an oval shaped segment of moderately firm*

8 hours x 7 days x 52 weeks x # of hospitals

        = how much fear?

*breast tissue measuring 3.4 x 2.6 x 1cm. . . . The cut
surfaces show moderately dense tan breast tissue.*

I can't bathe, I can't touch
the possibility of death
or survival
                wrapped in gauze like a sanitary pad
                I smell shame

my breasts nothing
                pathological examination

and everything

Death, Divorce, Resurrection

I.
She hadn't noticed any bruises
before her mother died. And she wasn't
really looking for them, now.
But, once or twice a day, she'd find herself touching
her right thigh, her left
breast, her vagina.

Her bruises were neither a death
threat, nor a death
wish. They were merely the first part
of herself she paid attention to.

II.
Did her mother's death release her?

She cried because no one else cried.
And didn't every dying mother deserve some tears?

Three hours with your mother's dead body in a hospital room
waiting for the last sibling to arrive,
enough time
to write a sermon.

III.
She sat at the airport waiting

realized, she was alone

IV.
happier than she'd ever been.
Damn happy.

But, could she trust the woman—her coffee, her kiss?

V.
She refused to believe her mother
haunted her.
She refused to believe

    death was the price of freedom.

She refused to believe love
could be wrong.

She refused to believe
she was writing fiction
    in the diary she never kept.

VI.
She had given the marriage twelve years.
Another year. Another month. Another week.
Did she know when it was over?

Was it her choice?

How many times had she said to her husband,
I love the most.

VII.
Ghirardelli chocolate always reminded her
she had another pimple on the tip of her nose.
Menopause was more like puberty than old age.
She wanted to dance.

Everyone hugs someone at airports. She wasn't leaving empty handed.

VIII.
She could have traded in her ticket, but
purple was and always had been
her favorite color.

Her bruises were never black and blue.

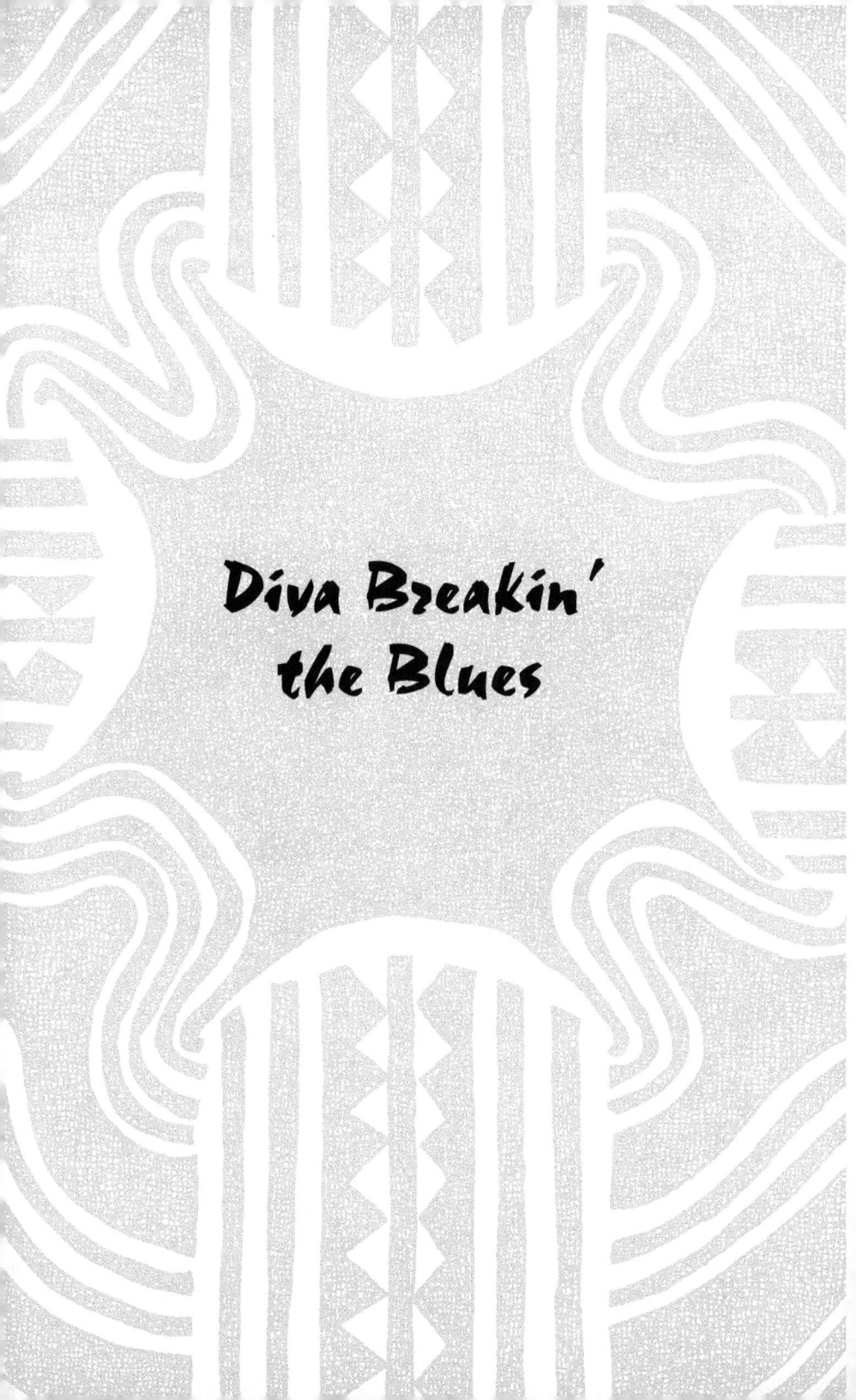

Diva Breakin' the Blues

China Doll

I am not a China doll. I am not a Geisha slut. I am not. Oriental. Exotic. Eastern. Fantasy. I'm not. I wear my mandarin collar, my frog closures for me. Because I can. Because I am. I wear my silk, my brocade. I am beautiful. Delicate. Okay, some stereotypes were me. Silent. Passive. Accommodating. Were me. Exotic. Were me. Were me.

I Will Divorce You

To the men—I have met
and will meet—
      I apologize.
I cannot

love you. Women
have appeared.

I have nothing
to write with. How

can I hold her. I spent
years searching,

      imagining

           he announces one of my pant legs is longer
           than the other one, explains I'm off balance

Silence
is a closed space secrets
rely on, hide and go
seek.

I must speak.

Verbs,

I can't waste
any of them.

She said,
Happiness

I believe
magic

markers

red

Diva Breakin' the Blues

        singin' the blues

           sweet singin' blues

                black lady blues

singin' sweetly

    like jasmine

        feelin' fine
          mind
          brilliant

  toes
   knees
  navel
    nipples
   neck
    ears
        kissed

soft moist lips

brown skin bright/
       grandma's quilt wrapped tight

    embracing

the blues

black lady blues

   blue lady

      no blues tonight
   black lady,
        lavish
        luscious
        lovely

Women Who Run

Go ahead. Run
26 miles or a life time.

I don't want to see
stamina, whether it
strengthens or weakens
which muscles
but, yes to the mind
unraveling
then tightening

> a ball of yarn—
> a sweater returned
> to its origin

> a new thought
> a scarf
> or mittens

is red a good color or gray?

a yes, a yes or a maybe

only god says no
to life and death

straight roads are narrow
go nowhere faster—

> run without me

marathons mark time—

       I will wait

knit one purl one wool or silk
my bamboo needles
stick—before I reach
an end
      or a conversation

sometimes I watch your journey
sometimes I have to watch mine

will the future burn or freeze?

We will know
when we satisfy
desire.

It Is Not Good

paying attention to detail.

The eye can mistake
a hand reaching for a hand
taking. A gloved hand
for a naked one.
Senorita, is your heart
breathing? or has my latest
cigarette choked us?
Is my hand of gold rings and purple
polish concrete
or abstract? Today I wander through old
poems, know
they have shown me
nothing.
Love cannot be observed

The hand is quicker than the eye

thus, my pen waits for the verb
to be active.

I can't rewrite my life
or finish this poem. I can search
smoldering ashes or
start a fire.

Naming

Family surnames all begin with S (except my dad's—Theun Wing).

Language sifts like sand through Chinese hands.

I spent six years in remedial speech classes. I was told
I couldn't pronounce the letter S.

I am fifty-four and still afraid—of my voice. Words jumble.

I stumble on last names. Each new husband
terrified me.

I hacked off the name of my last husband, was left
with my middle name Lee.

Lee is a Chinese name, so I won't get lost, but where is my mother?

I practice saying my prayers in front of cracked mirrors. Watch
lips part.

Love is never easy.

She named me from pieces of myself put back together. QuanLee.
The naming and the name both noisy.

No one else has given me such deep consonant sounds.

No one else has given me a body and a face.

I have trouble saying it sometimes.

No one else has touched me with her tongue untied.

No one else has interrupted desire to articulate love.

For her birthday I will not give trinkets or knickknacks that require dusting or discarding.

> I will whisper in her ear, *Quan Lee.*

> I will whisper in her ear.

Insomnia

1 Each night I come undone silk threads close to breaking.

2 I want so much
3 to touch her.

4 Tonight I know
5 I don't know
        6 how she feels

7 I've never felt
        8 so helpless

9 I can't stay
        10 this awake!

11 My friend says: *a poem must start in the world*
12 *before it becomes personal.*

13 Have I always done it wrong?

14 I tell my students to start with themselves
15 before entering the world; has anyone climbed
16 out of small windows

17 I think I'll just kiss her!

18 I wish she'd tell me to leave.
19 I wish she'd tell me she hates me.

20 I used to know who I was

21 perhaps I don't love women—perhaps I don't love me
22 perhaps I'm not the *fem* everyone says I am

23 perhaps I'm losing estrogen and I'm off kilter.

24 I knew the minute I saw her. I knew the year I chased her. I knew.

25 Whatever I did I undid it.

26 She gave me a small glimpse of herself, than retreated.
27 Has anyone climbed into small windows?

28 Yesterday I broke my mirror.

What Song is She Singing?

Pop the corn simmer the tea.

I've put lace curtains in the women's room,
dragons in the den

yellow roses everywhere

*I can't touch without wanting
can't touch without weeping*

                no one wants a clinging vine, a dead bird.

*Punish me for leaving, but don't punish me
for returning.*

          Did you know my first love was a neighborhood girl,
          blue eyes, blonde hair in a ponytail?

It's the woman I'm in love with

          Hands off. Teeth off.

the woman and the little girl.

      who should wear flannel? who should wear silk?

Heavy breathing keeps me awake.

      *Do you know what it is I need
      and when I need it?*

Sometimes pills work, or exhaustion, or red wine.

Do I need to be touched to know me?
Or do I need to be touched to know you?

She rolled over and said,
                "you were missing,
                        let me hold you,
                                come."

Apologies are no longer easy for me,
mostly, I am always tired.

I Asked My Husband if He Thought I Was a Lesbian and He Said, Yes

I met Love at a poetry reading. A lifetime of desire danced inches from the hard seat I was sitting on. She was like nothing imagined, nothing experienced.

I stopped writing. I started running. The Woman and I danced. The husband knew I was disappearing.

Ecstasy was a foreign intruder. I welcomed her. I closeted fifty years of living, went to the Woman in emperor's clothes.

A wise choice, joy despises mementos of fear and insecurity. But love is truth and truth finds its way out of closets all too quickly.

I tried on new clothes, starched shirts and creased pants. I wore silver bracelets. I gave away short skirts, and all my gold rings. I quit my job as a writer, swallowed my narrative.

Silence.

No more Matriarchal plantation stories, no more immigrant Chinese run-away father stories, no more Caucasian husband stories. Only the children survived. Only the sons who didn't deserve another episode of death and resurrection were allowed voice in my new covenant.

I was shameless. I told Barb, and Kris, and Eden, and Lee, and Corrine and so many other girl friends, I was in love with a woman. I even asked my husband, in another of my drunken stupors, if he thought I was a lesbian. He said, "yes."

Husbands were always white, always financially able—always available. They liked me sexy. They liked me smart. They liked me domestic. They liked me drunk. They were always gratuitous. I ate meat and potatoes. I lived in brick houses. I owned stuff.

But I always pushed the possibility of popping out of my masquerade which began when Mother said, "don't tell anyone you are Black. If they pester you, then tell them you are Chinese."

I thrust my feminist wiles, my racial/ethnic/cultural identities at my husbands' manhood. But they overlooked the shoving, exulting in the erotic, exotic, Black/Chinese Barbie doll Madonna/whore that I was nurtured to be. Husband after hedonistic white husband enjoyed associating with me, the marginalized. Because of course, I was trendy. Yet each hunkered down, holding their top dog position.

Husband number four was actually hit so hard and fast and frequently, he started to acquiesce. But, by then I was weathered and frigid. Twelve years of his limp white diction left me expressionless.

At fifty, I wasn't sure happiness, spelled l-o-v-e, was attainable. But I knew searching for love was against all probability of finding it. So I opened a space in my heart and my poems for love to happen.

I promised myself when love secreted her sensuous scent of lilacs blooming in the spring, I would succumb to her. No one would stop me from loving.

Ecstasy came the moment I saw her, before touching, before knowing, before committing. My friend said I was crying because *I was in love*. I ran toward love with a dozen boxes of Kleenex. I ran toward love, the poem, and the narrative. Ask anyone tangled on my journey how fast and far I ran. Only one intellectual friend, locked in her own bruised, brown body and spirit, cast me off as immoral.

But my son, who I fought for in patriarchal courtrooms so he could escape the suburbs and escape the step mother who explained to a mediator she understood racial complexity by stating "I told my daughters Michael was dark because he tanned darker than the rest of us"—

he said, "Mom, get a life. It's the new millenium. We love you. " This was the same dear son who told me years earlier, "it's okay that you write all that identity junk, but I know who I am, and I'm cool, I'm cool."

I ran for a year before I reached the Woman. Knee surgery slowed her running. But it's been heaven, and it's been hell, this love.

Love's first hug hints at responsibility. Love's first kiss reeks of commitment. Love doesn't last in a vacuum. It chews on memories. Spits out fear and insecurity to be reckoned with—to be cuddled and cauterized. My fears and insecurities/her fears and insecurities invaded the vacuum. Love tiptoed and tumbled, aggravated. Slugs wormed their way into our house of anxiety, leaving a trail of slime that constantly needed to be cleaned away.

The Woman I love has deep roots. She has grown into herself, a headstrong, handsome Chicana. She doesn't tolerate fragile or fluctuating branches. She waters her dreams nightly and every day her dreams come to fruition.

I am a thorn in her side. I keep on pinching. But, she doesn't allow herself to bleed.

She said that I was thin and shattered. She wouldn't tolerate the frenzy of flying glass. Nor did she want to super glue the broken pieces. She said "my demons are my demons and they are none of your business."

I said, "I really want you to know me."

After only four years of loving, suddenly, there was no love.
Cracked cement. Crushed stone.

So, again, I am writing:

> My mentor said it's not about being a good or bad writer.
> It's about: *keep writing*. It's about taking the writing deeper.
> It's about a psychological block.
> It's about wounds wrapped in a Black/Chinese/Female identity
> punctured again and again, and again,
> always festering, never healing:

- an African American mother passing for White
- a Chinese father divorcing a Black mother for a red-haired Polish woman
- Black relatives visiting at night so the neighbors couldn't see them
- lemon cream to keep your skin from getting dark(er)
- not going to the bathroom when you need to because you don't want to look in a mirror because you are ugly
- the in-laws who don't want mixed race grand babies
- the mother who says she will kill you if you get pregnant, insists you to take birth control pills
- the university program that told a student she would be the first Black Creative Writer to earn the M.F.A.—but you had already earned one!
- the seminary student whose parents won't let him marry you so he marries a woman from Japan
- the alcoholic husband who beats you in Boston, asks for a divorce because he says you are crazy, then marries a woman in California the day after you divorce him, then he approaches you in Minneapolis thirty years later because his third wife has left him and he wants to date you
- the step-children who don't have a clue, after twelve years of knowing you, that you aren't Japanese
- the mother who says, "a bad husband is better than no husband, you hear"
- the sixth grade teacher that won't let you sing

Being loved doesn't heal or hide wounds. Love discloses them. *Be the person you are, don't be the person you were when you were pretending not to be the person you were before which was the person pretending/and not pretending to be the person you were falsely nurtured to be.* I am an archive of charades.

Years of collecting wounds like a body full of tattoos may signify survival of a thousand needle pricks, but will never be memoir until a deeper understanding of the pain is revealed.

I am a fifty-four year-old Black/Chinese/Female/Poet; I sweat.

Marathon

She ran toward a ginger brown woman

caught the woman—inside out, charming

I melt, yellow squeezed from a black heart

wear wool gloves a red scarf cinches my mouth
I knit a hot fire of words

burn my tongue wanting

We danced in a closet with no air
the muse of a tango missing every other beat because

she was singing her song which kept repeating itself

I can still hear her needing my permission

and I ran (and I run) and sweat from the hot flashes
of maybe today the month thinning

or was the last violet hue of this rainbow
predicting a hard rain?

26.2 miles and 26.2 miles too many miles
we pray, then

 when war horrifies and haunts
 ghosts stock pile purified water and Ramen noodles.

We cry. Know touching and touch, loving and love
are memories and dreams of survival

Shameless, she kneels on stiff knees unforgiving;
angels usher me home

night is safe as day, and we are lonely

running was never an escape, just a statement.

Lotus petals pepper her breasts, who is kissing me?

She is the sweet succulent poem I have written

Yes, I taste tomorrow
                      my scarred tongue laughing

I Am the Snake I Feared

Coiled since birth, an unrelenting
fetal position. Mother chose
to keep me small. Each time

I tried unraveling, she scolded,
stay down, stay under, stay in.

She crossed her legs and held
me in her womb. Imagine

how my pushing pained her.
But *no* becomes a *yes*. White

is not a color, only distilled light
that blinds me.

So what if black embraces blue?
Blue is so suggestive.

I thank you woman, for all your *nos* and
all your *yeses*. No one else has stopped

the slithering spotted snake and
meant *I love you*.

Perhaps my mother's womb held
more than secrets. Perhaps

impatience is the snake
of who I am.

Today the snake spits afterbirth.
No arguments, no regrets.

Sometimes I think I'm whispering
when you complain I'm hissing.

I'm sorry if my wounds are noisy, but

I haven't left. I'm not leaving.
Only my thoughts wander

I am home, for the first time
in fifty-four years, venomless.

Some of the poems in this book appeared, some in slightly different versions or excerpts, in the following journals:

Asian American Renaissance, *Body of Stories,* Winter 2002, "I Asked My Husband if He Thought I Was a Lesbian and He Said, Yes"

Asian American Renaissance, *Spirits, Myths, and Dreams: Stories in Transit,* Summer/Fall 2000, "China Doll"

Asian American Renaissance, SexualORIENTations, 1999, "Reunion"

Colors, September/November 1995, "Diva Breakin' the Blues"

Drum Voices Review, Summer/Fall 2000, "Since I was Born"

A Woman's Place, Winter 1996, "I Will Divorce You"

About the Author

SHERRY QUAN LEE, author of *How to Write a Suicide Note* (2008) approaches writing as a community resource and as culturally based art of an ordinary everyday practical aesthetic. She is a Distinguished Alumni of North Hennepin Community College. Currently, she is the Program Associate for the Split Rock Arts Program summer workshops and the Online Mentoring for Writers Program at the University of Minnesota where she also earned her MFA in Creative Writing.

Recently retired from ten years of teaching Creative Writing at Metropolitan State University, Saint Paul, Minnesota, Quan Lee facilitates community workshops at Intermedia Arts, and elsewhere. She was a first year, 1996, participant of Cave Canem, a writing retreat for Black poets.

You can learn more about Sherry Quan Lee and view more of her work at www.SherryQuanLee.com.

www.ingramcontent.com/pod-product-compliance
Lightning Source LLC
Chambersburg PA
CBHW071743090426
42738CB00011B/2541